Highway To Heaven

Matthew 6:33 King James Version
But seek ye first the kingdom of God, and his righteousness;
and all these things shall be added unto you.

By Julie Kemp and Landon Whitley

Illustrated by Abira Das

In this amazing story of experiences in Heaven, it will give you comfort in knowing the beauty that awaits for all those that believe in Jesus.

Copyright © 2018 Julie Kemp and Landon Whitley
Illustrated by Abira Das
All rights reserved.

No part of this book may be reproduced in any manner without the written consent of the publisher except for brief excerpts in critical reviews or articles.

ISBN: 978-1-61244-680-6
Library of Congress Control Number: 2018961780

Printed in the United States of America

Halo Publishing International
1100 NW Loop 410
Suite 700 - 176
San Antonio, Texas 78213
Toll Free 1-877-705-9647
www.halopublishing.com
e-mail: contact@halopublishing.com

To my dad:
I know that God created man in His image.
And Dad, I am created in your image so you will always be a part of me.
I love you and I can't wait to see you in heaven again!

~Landon Whitley

When I was eight years old, I loved to play baseball and football. I had some really cool buddies, but my best friend was my dad. My dad was also my coach. We went hunting and fishing together. We rode four-wheelers and we watched wrestling.

A lot of our friends told us that wrestling was fake, but we watched it anyway. Every Monday night, we would yell at the TV screen during the World Wrestling Federation. My dad would even let me stay up late on school nights to watch it with him.

Baseball is my favorite sport. I always wear jersey #11. I chose that number because it was my dad's number when he played baseball. My dad is my hero.

One day on our way home from church, my family was involved in a terrible car accident. My dad went to heaven. Nobody told me that he went there. I just knew it because I saw him there. I went to heaven too. It was the first time I had been to heaven. It was not scary and I was not sad.

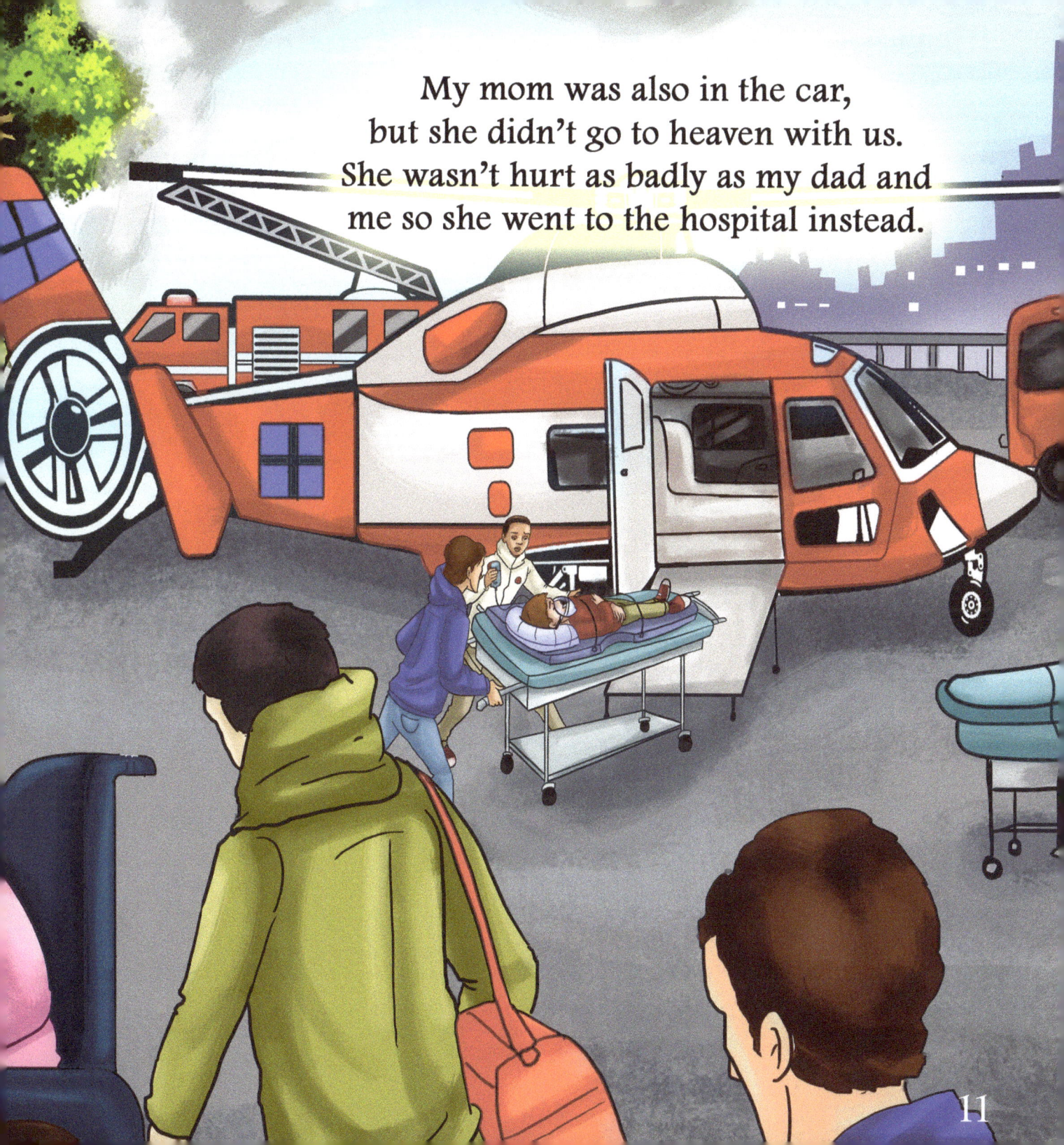

My mom was also in the car, but she didn't go to heaven with us. She wasn't hurt as badly as my dad and me so she went to the hospital instead.

The second time I went to heaven,
I saw a brother and a sister that
I didn't even know I had. For some reason,
they hadn't lived for very long in our mom's belly.
But they were definitely alive in heaven!

Heaven is a beautiful place. It is so bright. Imagine all your favorite colors, then mix them together and shine them under a magnifying glass.

Heaven is bigger and brighter than any rainbow you've ever seen!

There are angels in heaven.
They really like to sing and dance.
They are very happy. It is amazing how beautiful they are. Their music is loud and they are praising Jesus.

The angels are dressed differently than the other people in heaven who are called saints. You can tell the difference between the angels and the saints.

The third time I went to heaven, I got to see Jesus. I especially liked spending time with Him. I was very happy to be in heaven with my dad and Jesus. Jesus told me, "You have to go back to earth and be a good Christian and tell others about Me."

I wanted to beg to stay, but I knew I couldn't argue with Jesus, even though no one had told me that. I just knew I had to obey and come back to earth.

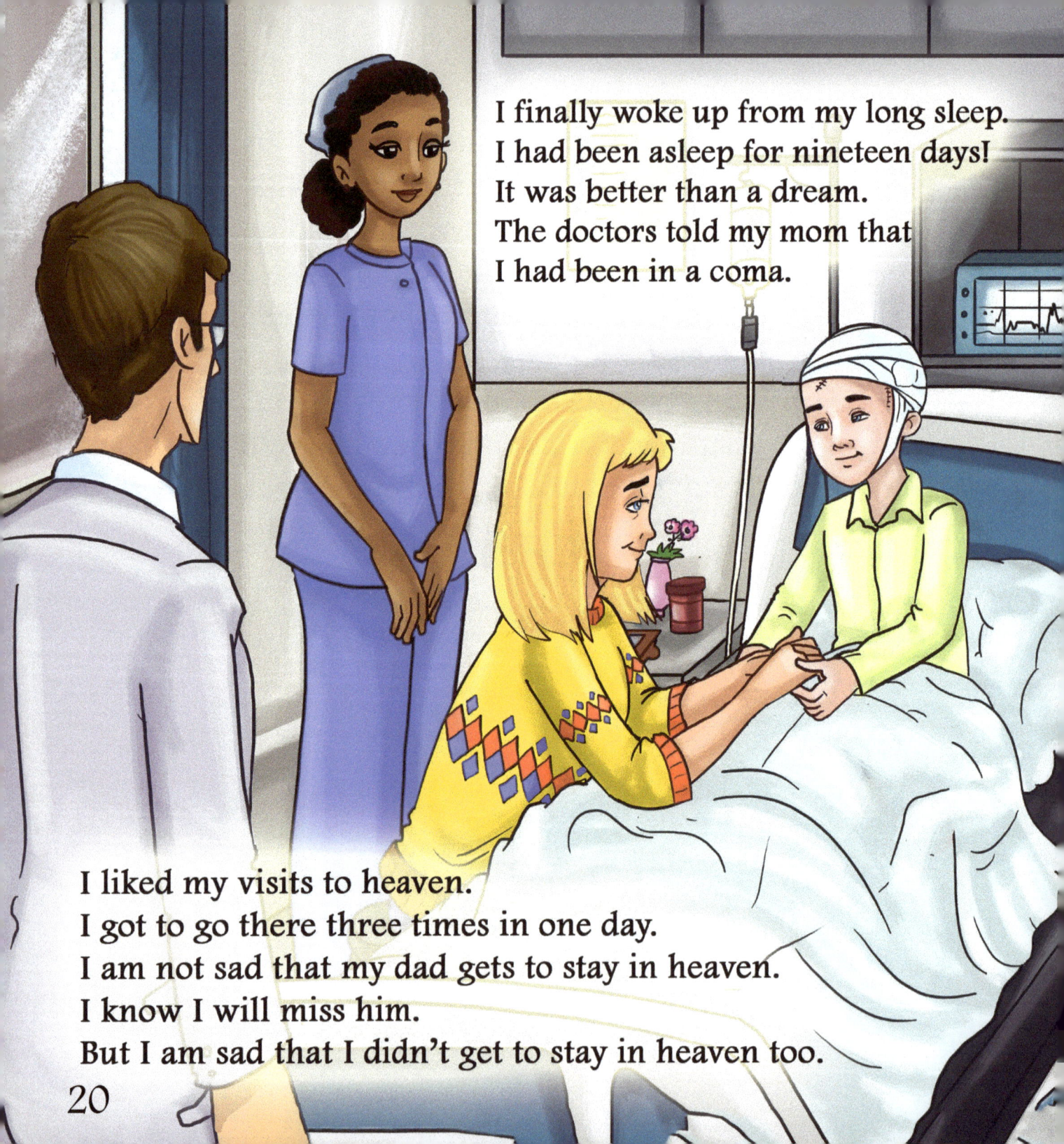

I finally woke up from my long sleep.
I had been asleep for nineteen days!
It was better than a dream.
The doctors told my mom that
I had been in a coma.

I liked my visits to heaven.
I got to go there three times in one day.
I am not sad that my dad gets to stay in heaven.
I know I will miss him.
But I am sad that I didn't get to stay in heaven too.

If your best friend, your hero, your mom,
or your dad has gone to heaven, try not to be too sad.
They are happy. Everyone gets a new body in heaven,
and nobody is sick. I know that you will miss those you love.
But believe in Jesus and you will get to live with them and
Jesus forever—when it is your turn.

The week before our accident, I was sitting in my classroom and my teacher gave us an assignment. She asked all the students to draw a picture of what we thought heaven would look like. I drew a pearly gate. I thought that after I went through the pearly gates, I would walk on streets of gold. That part was right. There really are streets of gold in heaven. I drew an orange mansion, although it was not very big in my picture. I also included the river of life. If you're wondering why I put a tree on my picture, it was because I thought my dad and I would need one to go deer hunting in heaven.

What do you think heaven will look like?

Remember, when you draw your picture of heaven, use the brightest colors you have. And include your loved one—whoever that may be.

While I am not a famous person, I do feel pretty special. After all, I feel like I have an angel in the outfield who is with me at every ballgame.

The famous actor that I was named after is Michael Landon. He starred in a show called "Highway to Heaven." My parents didn't know when they named me that I would have my own highway to heaven.

Dear Jesus,
I pray for all my friends who are sad.
Please make their hearts happy again.
Will You comfort and love them while
filling their thoughts with wonderful
memories? I know You are taking great
care of their loved ones in heaven.

In the Bible, it says "For God so loved
the world that He gave His one and
only Son, that whoever believes in Him
shall not perish but have eternal life."
(John 3:16)

Thank You for keeping
all Your promises!

Amen

www.ingramcontent.com/pod-product-compliance
Lightning Source LLC
Chambersburg PA
CBHW041438040426
42453CB00021B/2459